D1682480

Exploring WORLD LANDMARKS

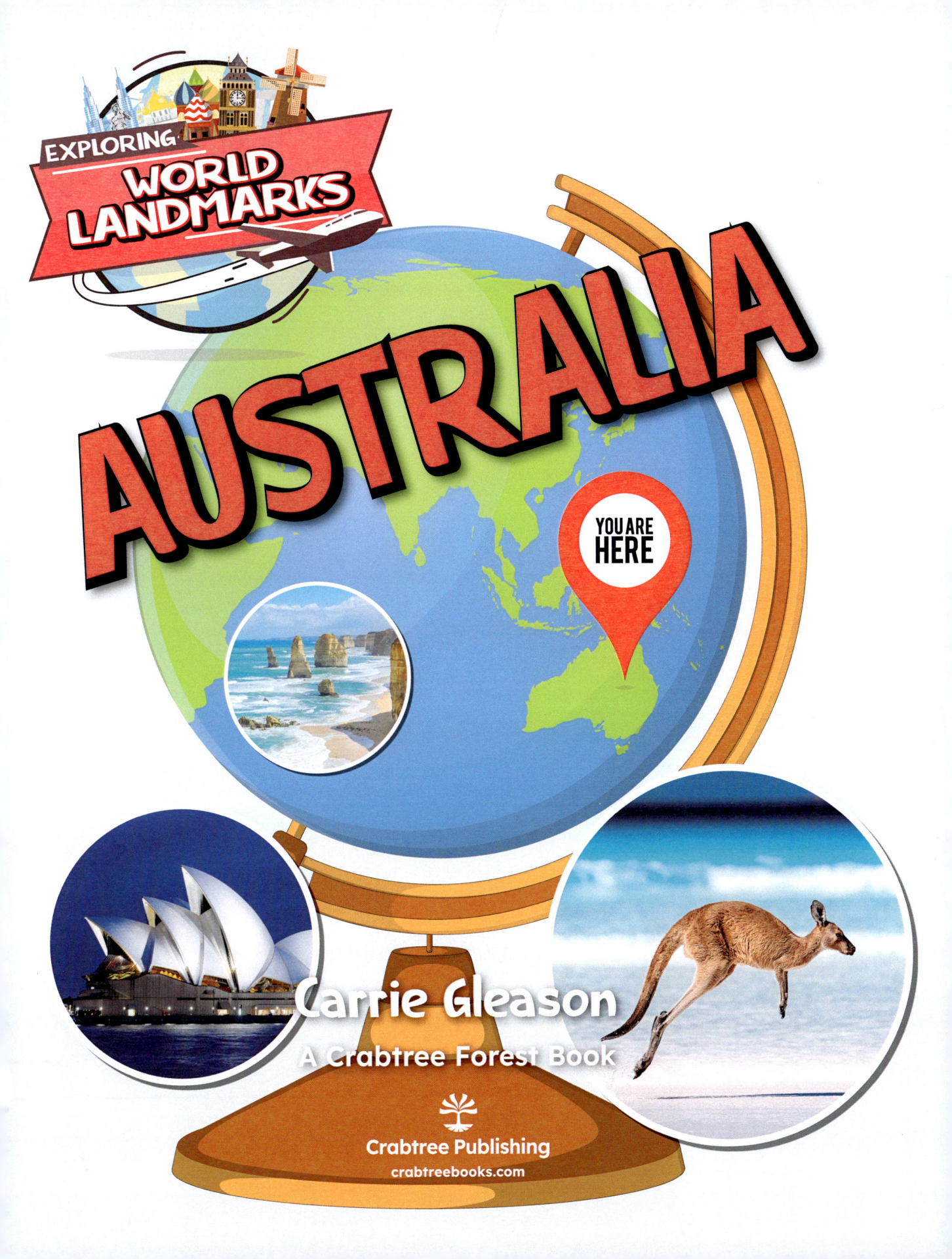

AUSTRALIA

YOU ARE HERE

Carrie Gleason

A Crabtree Forest Book

Crabtree Publishing
crabtreebooks.com

Developed and produced by Plan B Book Packagers
www.planbbookpackagers.com
Art director: Rosie Gowsell Pattison
Author: Carrie Gleason
Crabtree editor: Ellen Rodger
Prepress technician: Margaret Salter
Production coordinator: Katherine Berti
Proofreader: Crystal Sikkens
Photographs:
All images from Shutterstock.com

Crabtree Publishing

crabtreebooks.com 800-387-7650
Copyright © 2024 Crabtree Publishing
All rights reserved. No part of this publication may be reproduced, stored in a retrieval system or be transmitted in any form or by any means, electronic, mechanical, photocopying, recording, or otherwise, without the prior written permission of Crabtree Publishing. In Canada: We acknowledge the financial support of the Government of Canada through the Canada Book Fund for our publishing activities.

Hardcover   978-1-0398-1535-3
Paperback   978-1-0398-1561-2
Ebook (pdf)   978-1-0398-1613-8
Epub   978-1-0398-1587-2

Published in Canada
Crabtree Publishing
616 Welland Avenue
St. Catharines, Ontario
L2M 5V6

Published in the United States
Crabtree Publishing
347 Fifth Avenue
Suite 1402-145
New York, NY 10016

Library and Archives Canada Cataloguing in Publication
Available at the Library and Archives Canada

Library of Congress Cataloging-in-Publication Data
Available at the Library of Congress

Printed in the U.S.A./022024/PP20240115

Contents

Next Stop: Australia! .... page 4

Sydney Opera House .... page 6

Uluru .... page 8

Great Barrier Reef .... page 10

Parliament House .... page 12

The Three Sisters .... page 14

Port Arthur .... page 16

Bondi Beach .... page 18

Eureka Tower .... page 20

Bungle Bungles .... page 22

Shark Bay .... page 24

Sydney Harbour Bridge .... page 26

Burke and Willis Dig Tree .... page 28

The Big Merino .... page 30

Kakadu Rock Art .... page 32

Twelve Apostles .... page 34

Royal Exhibition Building .... page 36

Wave Rock .... page 38

Australian War Memorial .... page 40

Gwalia Ghost Town .... page 42

Billabongs .... page 44

Australia at a Glance .... page 46

Glossary .... page 47

Learning More .... page 48

Index .... page 48

Next Stop: Australia!

G'day mate! Welcome to Australia. Australia is known for its ancient landforms, unique animals, sunny beaches, and modern cities. In this book you will find some of Australia's most important landmarks.

FIVE Australia Facts

1. Australia is the sixth-largest country in the world.

2. Australia's Indigenous peoples arrived there about 65,000 years ago from southeast Asia. There are two main groups—Aboriginal Australians and Torres Strait Islanders—with many individual nations within them.

3. Australia is nicknamed "Oz" or the "Land Down Under." People who live there are sometimes called "Aussies."

4. Most Australians live in cities along the east coast. The Outback, a large rural area that includes deserts and bush, lies in the center of the country.

5. Kangaroos, koala bears, platypuses, and Tasmanian devils are just a few of the animals that are only found in Australia.

Shark Bay

WESTERN AUSTRALIA

Gwalia Ghost Town

Wave Rock

WHAT IS A LANDMARK?

Landmarks are unique natural or human-made structures that tell us where in the world we are. In your neighborhood, a landmark might be a large tree in the center of town, a special building, or a park. Countries also have landmarks, but on a much bigger scale. Examples of landmarks might be large mountains and waterfalls, ancient buildings and statues, and modern bridges and towers.

MAP OF AUSTRALIA

This map shows the shape of Australia. Australia is divided into 6 states and 10 territories. The general location of the landmarks in this book are shown on the map.

Kakadu Rock Art
Bungle Bungles
NORTHERN TERRITORY
Uluru
Great Barrier Reef
QUEENSLAND
Billabongs
Burke and Willis Dig Tree
SOUTH AUSTRALIA
NEW SOUTH WALES
Sydney Opera House
The Big Merino
Three Sisters
Sydney Harbour Bridge
Royal Exhibition Building
AUSTRALIAN CAPITAL REGION
Bondi Beach
VICTORIA
Eureka Tower
Parliament House
Australian War Memorial
Twelve Apostles
TASMANIA
Port Arthur

5

Sydney Opera House

Jutting into Sydney Harbour, the Sydney Opera House looks like a bunch of seashells floating on water. This huge performing arts center includes several concert halls where operas, ballets, and symphony concerts take place. The Opera House is Australia's best-known landmark—and it almost didn't get built! It took ten years longer than expected to finish and cost millions of dollars more than people thought it would. A number of problems had to be solved while building this one-of-a-kind structure.

At first, the underwater posts supporting the platform on which it rests weren't strong enough and had to be replaced. Then, the columns for the roof weren't right and had to be rebuilt. Finally, engineers had to figure out how to make the large, white roof shells, or sails, which they did with the help of computers. This was back in the 1960s—before computers were used in engineering. The Sydney Opera House is a source of great pride for Australians. It proves that anything is possible, even the impossible!

In this picture, the shells of the Sydney Opera House have been lit up at night using projectors to show images of sea life.

Uluru

Uluru is a massive sandstone rock in the center of Australia. It is 1,142 feet (348 m) tall, which is almost as tall as the Empire State Building in New York. But that's only part of Uluru. Like an iceberg, most of it is hidden beneath the surface, where it continues for more than 1.5 miles (2.5 km) below ground. Geologists believe that Uluru was created between 500 and 300 million years ago when sediment built up, formed into rock, and then rose up from the surface due to movement of Earth's plates. The Indigenous people of the area, the Anangu, tell a different story of how the rock came to be. They believe it was created by spirits at the beginning of time. For them, Uluru, and the area around it, is a sacred place.

(background) Geologists call Uluru an "inselberg," which is a rock or hill in a flat area that looks kind of like an island on land.

8

(above) Uluru is an orange red color because of a mineral called iron in the rock. When iron is exposed to air, it rusts, giving the rock its color.

(right) Uluru is filled with caves shaped by wind and water wearing away the rock. Rainwater sometimes collects in the caves, making watering holes for people and animals in this arid, or dry, land.

9

Great Barrier Reef

The Great Barrier Reef is not only Australia's best-known natural landmark, it is also important to the entire planet. The many sea plants of the reef area help absorb a gas called carbon dioxide from the atmosphere, keeping the planet healthy. The reef was built over a period of about 20 million years from the skeletons of tiny ocean animals called polyps. It provides a home for a great variety of ocean life and protects the shore from waves and storms. For Australia, the Great Barrier Reef is important for fishing and tourism. More than a million people visit it each year to go scuba diving, snorkeling, and boating.

(left) Six of the seven types of sea turtles in the world can be found in the Great Barrier Reef. The reef provides protection from predators, food, and nearby beaches where the turtles lay their eggs.

(above) The Great Barrier Reef is 1,420 miles (2,300 km) long, and is the longest reef in the world. It lies off the coast of the state of Queensland, in northeast Australia.

FIVE
Reef Facts

1. The Great Barrier Reef is the largest living structure on Earth.

2. It is one of the Seven Natural Wonders of the World.

3. It is made up of 3,000 individual reefs, 980 islands, and countless mangrove forests near the shores.

4. Twenty-five percent of the world's marine species can be found there, including sharks, fish, rays, giant clams, and many more!

5. It can be seen from space!

Parliament House

Australia's Parliament House is nested in its home on Capital Hill, in Canberra. It is a low building with sloping grass sides that people can walk up to get to the roof. The government chose this design for the parliament buildings because they didn't want it to seem like the government was lording over its citizens by making a tall, grand structure. Two large curved walls shaped like boomerangs separate the different areas of the building. Boomerangs have special meaning for Indigenous Australians. They have been used for thousands of years as tools for hunting and digging, and as trade items. A tall flag pole rises from the top of Parliament House and can be seen from many miles around.

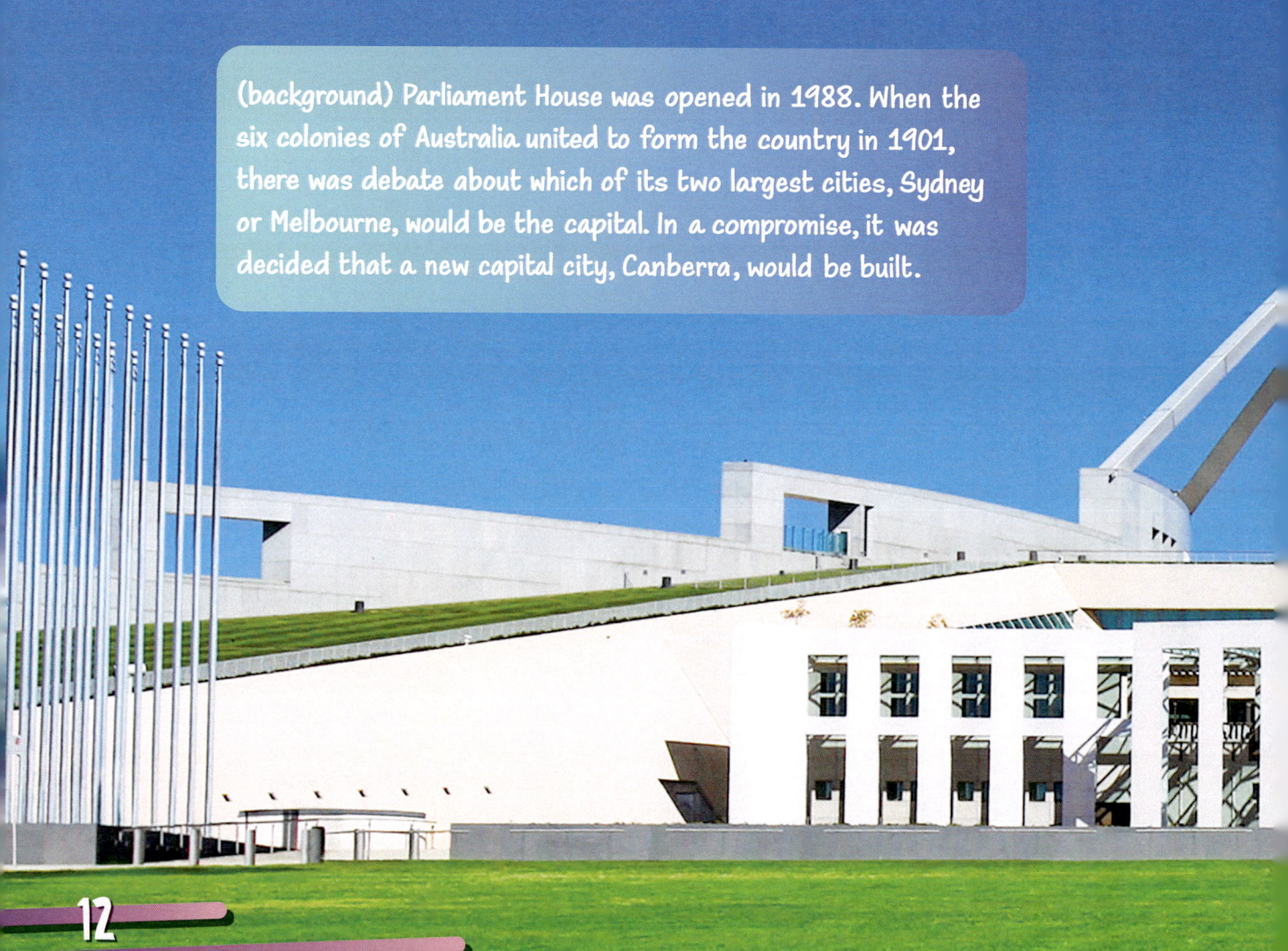

(background) Parliament House was opened in 1988. When the six colonies of Australia united to form the country in 1901, there was debate about which of its two largest cities, Sydney or Melbourne, would be the capital. In a compromise, it was decided that a new capital city, Canberra, would be built.

(above) A mosaic called "Possum and Wallaby Dreaming" decorates the entrance to Parliament House. It was created using 90,000 small pieces of granite rock. The mosaic is based on a painting by famous Indigenous Warlpiri artist Michael Nelson Jagamara. The secret to the meaning behind this artwork, like many creation stories, is kept by Aboriginal Australians.

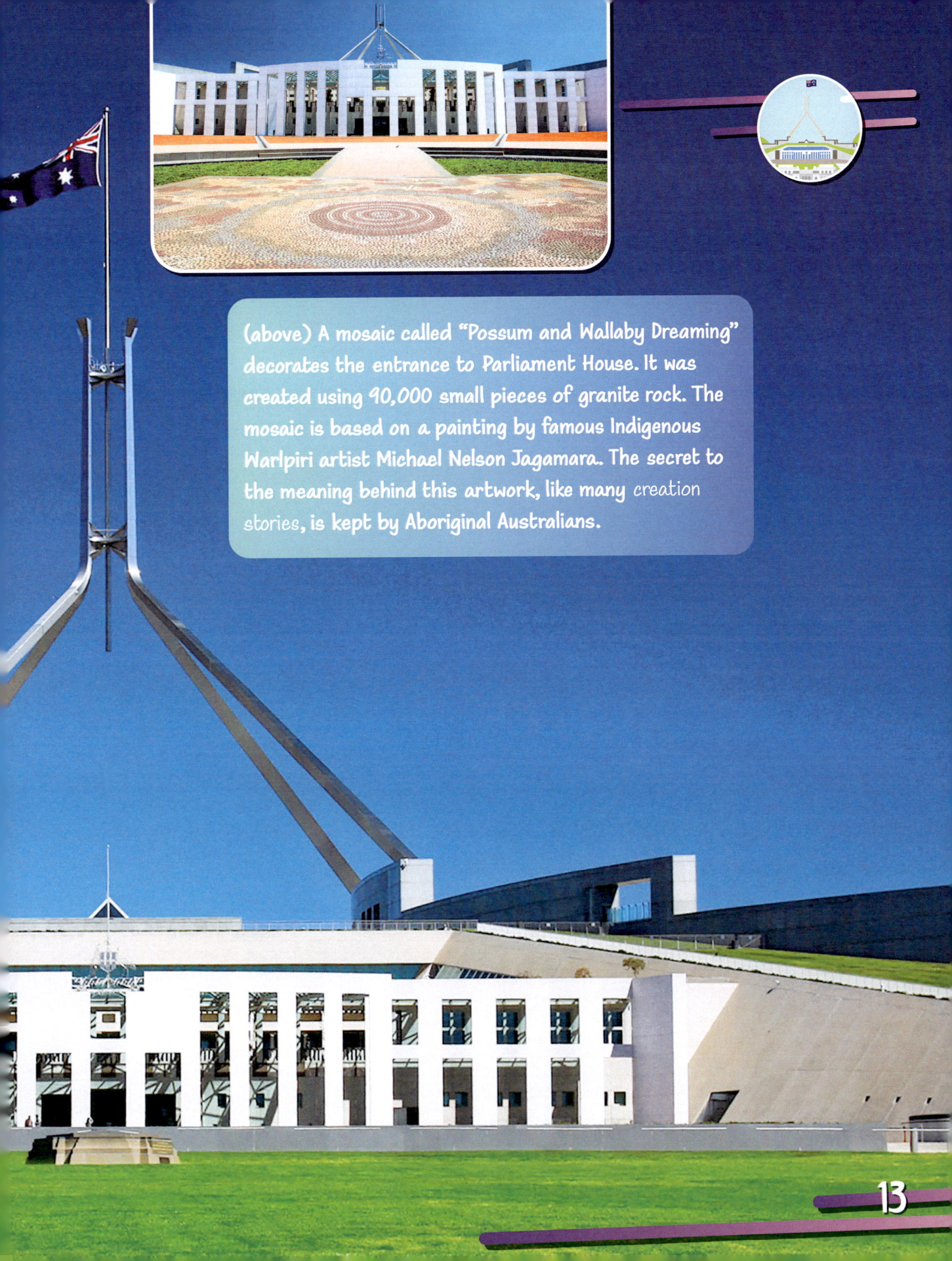

The Three Sisters

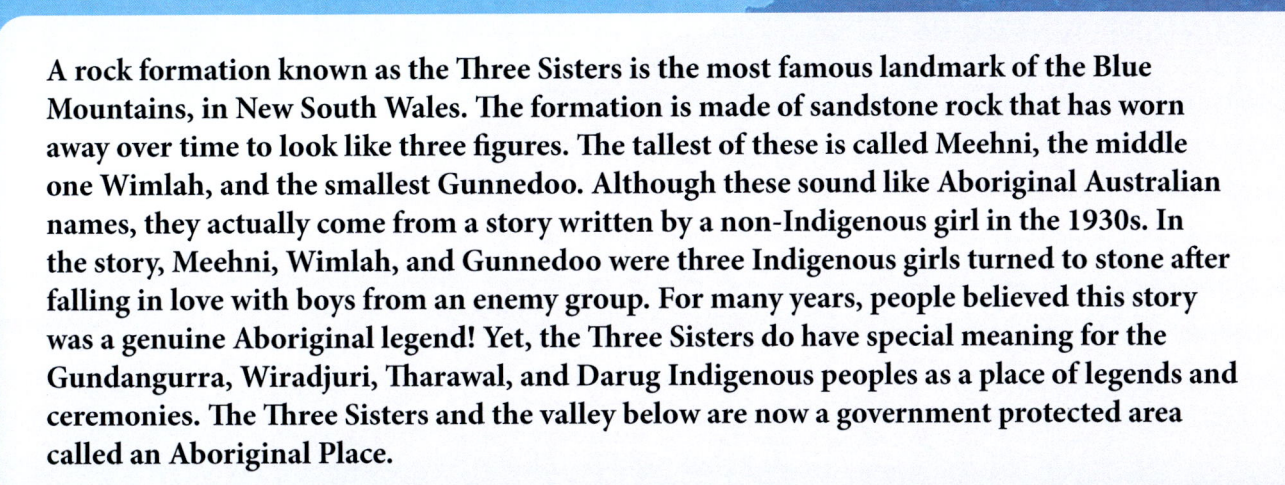

A rock formation known as the Three Sisters is the most famous landmark of the Blue Mountains, in New South Wales. The formation is made of sandstone rock that has worn away over time to look like three figures. The tallest of these is called Meehni, the middle one Wimlah, and the smallest Gunnedoo. Although these sound like Aboriginal Australian names, they actually come from a story written by a non-Indigenous girl in the 1930s. In the story, Meehni, Wimlah, and Gunnedoo were three Indigenous girls turned to stone after falling in love with boys from an enemy group. For many years, people believed this story was a genuine Aboriginal legend! Yet, the Three Sisters do have special meaning for the Gundangurra, Wiradjuri, Tharawal, and Darug Indigenous peoples as a place of legends and ceremonies. The Three Sisters and the valley below are now a government protected area called an Aboriginal Place.

Indigenous stories and legends are sacred to the people to which they belong. Indigenous Australians are working with the government today to reclaim sites, such as the Three Sisters, that have special meaning for them.

Port Arthur

Hundreds of years ago, the Tasmanian town of Port Arthur was used as a massive jail site. The ruins of the jail site, known as Port Arthur Penal Colony, are preserved on the island state 150 miles (240 km) off the coast of mainland Australia. The British began transporting, or shipping, convicted criminals to mainland Australia in 1778. Tasmania was even more remote. Convicts were sent there from 1803 to 1853. Once in Australia, they were put to work to build and feed the colony. When they had served their time, the convicts were set free and many made Australia their home. Those who committed more crimes after being freed were sent to secondary penal colonies, such as the one at Port Arthur. About 160,000 men, women, and boy convicts were sent to Australia from England and Ireland.

(background) The ruins of the large building in this photo was the penitentiary, where convicts lived. There were 30 buildings at the Port Arthur Penal Colony. They included a chapel, barracks and homes for guards and soldiers, a secondary prison for troublesome inmates, and an asylum where prisoners driven mad by punishment were kept.

(left) From the Guard Tower, soldiers kept watch for prisoners trying to escape. The stones used to build the tower were cut by teenage boys from a nearby boys' prison.

(left) At the Port Arthur historic site, people today can walk halls lined with prisoner's cells, and see what the inside of the prison was like.

17

Bondi Beach

Bondi Beach in Sydney is one of more than 10,000 sandy white beaches in Australia. It is Australia's most popular beach and home of the country's oldest surf clubs and swimming schools. The crescent-shaped beach is half a mile (1 km) long and meets the clear blue water of the Pacific Ocean. Because of Australia's warm climate, the beach is used year-round, but it is busiest in the summer months. Summer in Australia is from January to March.

(background) About 1,640 feet (500 m) from shore, shark nets have been set up to help protect swimmers and surfers from great white, tiger, and bull sharks.

(above) The Bondi Baths is a large swimming pool built on the edge of the beach.

(right) Australia is known for its surf culture. Many world champion surfers are from Australia. Surfing was introduced to the country in 1915 by a Hawaiian surfer named Duke Kahanamoku.

Eureka Tower

The Eureka Tower is a skyscraper in Melbourne, Victoria. The tower is named after the Eureka Rebellion of 1854, in which gold miners rose up against the colonial government. A gold rush had begun when gold was discovered there four years earlier. About 6,000 gold miners arrived in the area each week hoping to get rich. Unhappy with having to pay a tax to search for gold, a group of miners built a stockade. The miners wanted a fair say in government if they had to pay the tax. In 1854, colonial soldiers attacked the stockade, killing 22 miners. The Eureka Tower was designed to honor this event, which led to a fairer system of government in Australia.

(right) The Melbourne Skydeck is on the 88th floor of the tower. From its windows, people can see the city below.

(background) The golden rectangle at the top of the tower represents gold mining. The horizontal white stripes are meant to look like a leveling rod, a tool used when searching for gold, and the red stripe represents the blood that was shed during the rebellion.

21

Bungle Bungles

Rising out of the grasslands in northwest Australia are orange and black beehive-shaped hills known as the Bungle Bungles. They are made from a type of rock called sandstone. This was formed over long periods of time as layers of sand and sediment were squeezed together to form rock. Some of the stripes are orange. These areas have higher amounts of the mineral iron in them, which turns orange when exposed to the oxygen in the air. The black stripes are formed in parts that have more clay, and are actually colonies of tiny living things called cyanobacteria. When it rains, the cyanobacteria come to life and the stripes on the Bungle Bungles are brighter.

(background) The Bungle Bungles were a world secret for millions of years! Until 40 years ago, only the Indigenous Karjaganujaru people and ranchers knew about them. When the rest of the country found out about them, a national park called Purnululu was created around these hills.

(left) There are many passageways between the hills, creating a sort of maze.

23

Shark Bay

Shark Bay was given its name by English explorer William Dampier, who landed there in 1699. Although it is named for the many sharks he saw there, it is an important habitat for bottlenose dolphins, rays, turtles, and dugongs. Shark bay lies off the westernmost point of Australia. The water here is one-and-a-half times saltier than the rest of the oceans, which makes it extra special as one of a very few places where Earth's earliest life forms still grow. Stromatolites are layered sedimentary rock formations created by these microorganisms. Sand and other minerals stick to the microorganisms and grow layer by layer over time. Stromatolites have been around for billions of years and are sometimes called living fossils.

(background and above) The darker parts of the water in this photo show seagrass meadows. Shark Bay has the world's largest seagrass meadows. Many ocean animals, including dugongs, make seagrass meadows their homes.

(below) Guitarfish, also called guitar sharks, are one type of ray found in Shark Bay.

24

(below) Large pods of bottlenose dolphins live in Shark Bay.

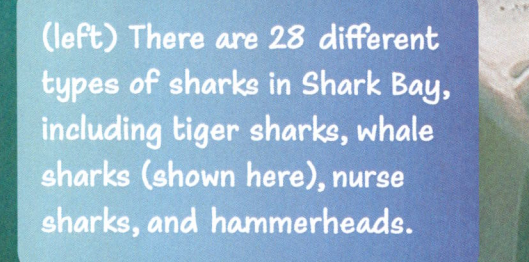

(left) There are 28 different types of sharks in Shark Bay, including tiger sharks, whale sharks (shown here), nurse sharks, and hammerheads.

(right) A sea of stromatolites in Shark Bay. The microorganisms in these rocks produce oxygen.

25

Sydney Harbour Bridge

Together with the Sydney Opera House, the Sydney Harbour Bridge is an important urban landmark in Australia. It is the tallest steel arch bridge in the world, and was a huge success when it was finished in 1932. To build the bridge, 550,000 pieces of steel were used, most of it brought over from England. To hold the steel pieces together, fasteners called rivets were used. For Australia, the bridge symbolized its progress from colony to modern country.

The Sydney Harbour Bridge has seven lanes for automobiles, as well as two lanes for trains, a lane for cyclists, and one for pedestrians.

27

Burke and Willis Dig Tree

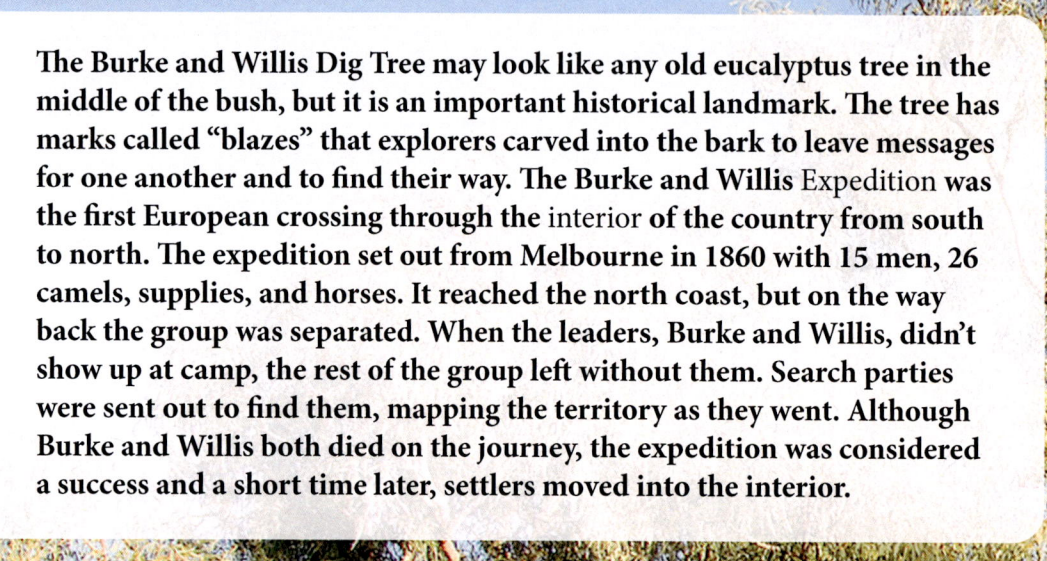

The Burke and Willis Dig Tree may look like any old eucalyptus tree in the middle of the bush, but it is an important historical landmark. The tree has marks called "blazes" that explorers carved into the bark to leave messages for one another and to find their way. The Burke and Willis Expedition was the first European crossing through the interior of the country from south to north. The expedition set out from Melbourne in 1860 with 15 men, 26 camels, supplies, and horses. It reached the north coast, but on the way back the group was separated. When the leaders, Burke and Willis, didn't show up at camp, the rest of the group left without them. Search parties were sent out to find them, mapping the territory as they went. Although Burke and Willis both died on the journey, the expedition was considered a success and a short time later, settlers moved into the interior.

(left) In 1898, a traveling artist and photographer named John Dick visited the site of the Burke and Willis camp and carved this image of Burke into a nearby tree to commemorate **him**.

(background) The men waiting for Burke and Willis blazed the word "DIG" into this tree. It was used to signal the location of supplies they had buried nearby. Burke and Willis did return to camp, but had missed the others by just nine hours.

The Big Merino

Dotted across the vast, open country are landmarks that Australians call "Big Things." These giant statues symbolize something that an area is known for. The first Big Thing was the Big Banana. It was built in the 1960s near a banana plantation in New South Wales. It was a big hit with Australians on road trips. Soon other Big Things started popping up around the country, such as the Big Merino, in Goulburn, New South Wales. Nicknamed "Rambo," this giant ram statue stands for sheep ranching in the area. Australia is the world's largest producer of sheep and wool.

FIVE Big Things

1 The Big Koala, or "Sam," is a gift shop in Dadswells Bridge, Victoria. It was named after a real-life koala that died after a bushfire. It was meant to raise awareness of the danger of bushfires to koalas.

2 The Big Lobster, or "Larry the Lobster" is in Kingston, South Australia. The idea for the statue came from a local lobster fisherman.

3 The Big Pineapple is on the Sunshine Coast in the northeast, where most of Australia's pineapples are grown.

4 The Big Mango in Bowen, Queensland, was made because of the mango orchards there.

5 The Big Prawn was built to honor the prawn fishing industry in Ballina, New South Wales. While the largest real-life prawns weigh about 5 ounces (150 g), the Big Prawn weighs as much as six elephants!

(background) The Big Merino is 50 feet (15 m) tall. There are stairs inside that visitors can climb up to look out the ram's eyes.

Kakadu Rock Art

Rock art at Kakadu National Park in the Northern Territory traces the long history of the local Bininj and Mungguy Indigenous peoples. The site is believed to be one of the first human settlements in Australia. The paintings on two large rock formations in the park, called Ubirr and Nourlangie, show the peoples' way of living over thousands of years, including the animals they hunted for food, contact with settlers, and creation stories.

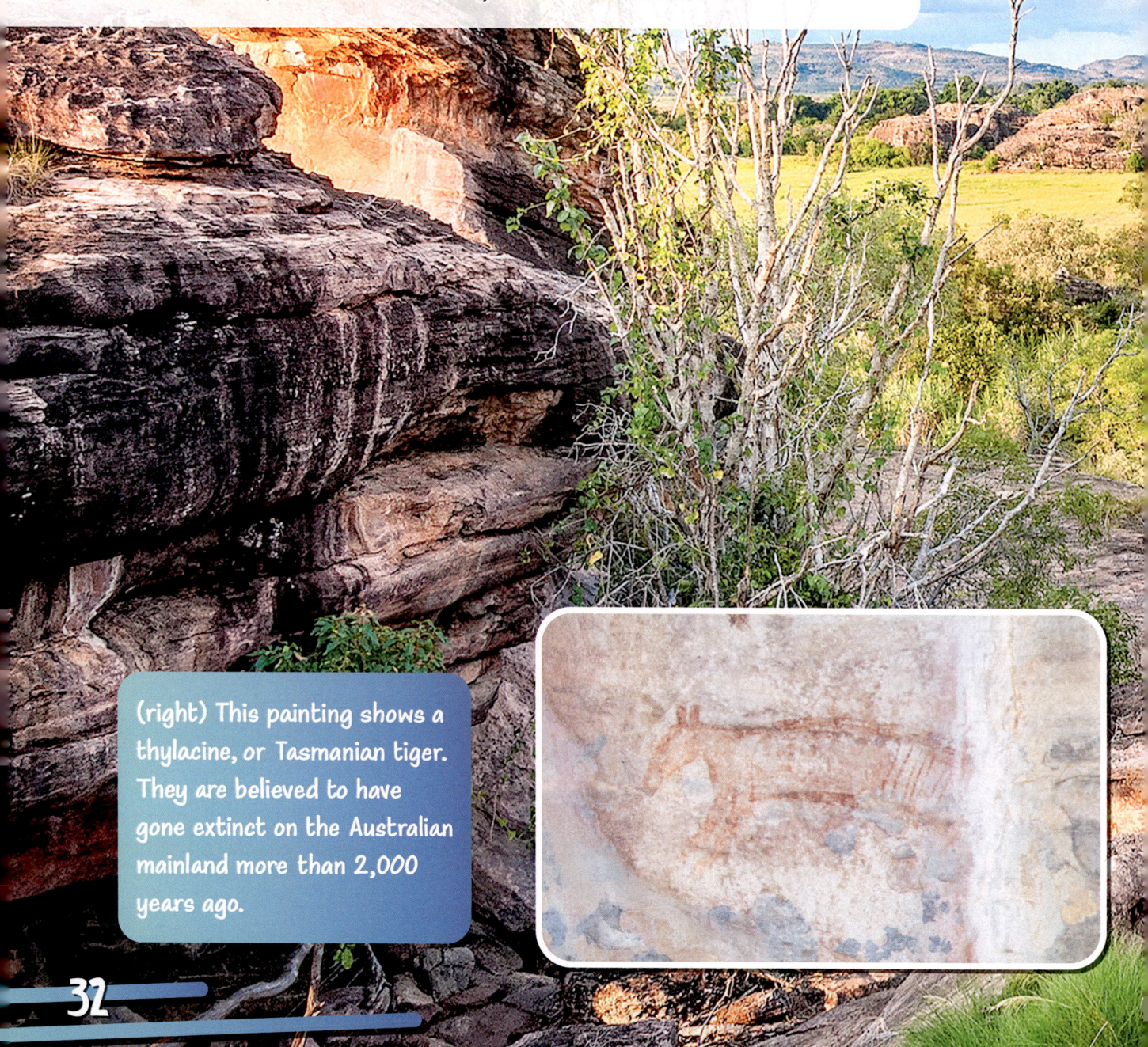

(right) This painting shows a thylacine, or Tasmanian tiger. They are believed to have gone extinct on the Australian mainland more than 2,000 years ago.

(left) This painting shows Namarrgon, or "Lightning Man," a mythical being who brings the start of the wet season.

(right) This painting is of Mabuyu, a hunter, who has a bag of fish and a spear for catching them.

(left) This fish painting is an example of x-ray art, in which the insides of the animal are shown in a decorative style.

33

Twelve Apostles

People driving on Australia's Great Ocean Road in southeast Australia will find the Twelve Apostles lining the ocean cliffs. The Twelve Apostles are made of limestone rock, which formed over millions of years from the skeletons of dead sea creatures. The stacks were once connected to the cliffs, but over time the waves and storms of the Southern Ocean created arches. When the arches collapsed, only the stacks were left standing.

Although they are called the Twelve Apostles, there are only seven stacks still standing today.

35

Royal Exhibition Building

Between 1851 and 1914, international exhibitions were world-class events where countries showed off their inventions and achievements. The Royal Exhibition Building was built for the 1880–81 Melbourne Exhibition. Although the fancy building had fallen into disrepair by the 1950s, it has been fixed up and today it is one of the last great exhibition buildings from the 1800s still standing. Through its history, the building has been used as the place where the first Australian parliament was opened in 1901, a hospital during the 1919 Spanish flu outbreak, as barracks and a training center for the air force during WWII, and for sports events during the 1956 Summer Olympic Games.

(background) A fountain and gardens sit outside the Royal Exhibition Building in Melbourne.

(above) The inside of the building has been restored to look like it did when it was first built. Today it is used for art exhibits, garden and other shows, and as a place where nearby college students write tests.

37

Wave Rock

(left) Close to Wave Rock is another interesting granite rock formation called Hippo's Yawn.

The town of Hyden, in Western Australia, is 120 miles (190 km) away from the ocean, but it is known for its giant ocean wave. This wave is not made of water, but from granite rock! The Wave Rock is 46 feet (14 m) high and 360 feet (110 m) long—about as long as a NFL football field. It is located on the side of a cliff and was formed by water and weather **eroding** the stone into the shape of a wave.

(background) It has taken about 2,700 million years for the Wave Rock to get its shape.

Australian War Memorial

The Australian War Memorial is a cross-shaped structure built in 1941. But it is more than a concrete cenotaph and statues used to honor the war dead once a year. It's a museum, parade grounds, park, and sculpture gardens that attracts visitors and scholars year round. Every year on April 25, Anzac Day, Australians remember fallen soldiers with services at dawn at the War Memorial.

(above) This sculpture honors members of the Australian navy who fought in wars.

40

(left) This sculpture commemorates the role of explosive detection dogs, used to sniff out bombs, and their handlers during wars.

(background) The idea to build a war memorial came about after WWI (1914-1918). As a member of the British Commonwealth, Australia joined the war when Great Britain declared war on Germany.

41

Gwalia Ghost Town

When gold was discovered in Gwalia, Western Australia, in 1896, people quickly rushed in to work in the mine. When the mine closed 24 years later, they all rushed out just as fast! Today, all that remains is an eerie, empty ghost town, with people's belongings still in some of the houses. At its peak, the little town had 1,200 people and a working school, public pool, tramway, and hotel. Today, visitors to the area can see life as it was during Australia's gold rush. They can also visit the former home of Herbert Hoover, a man who ran the mine, and later became the 31st president of the United States!

(background) This photo shows some of the abandoned homes in the Gwalia Ghost Town, a former mining town that now sits almost empty.

(above) The inside of a miner's home in Gwalia. Within three weeks of the mine closing, the population of the town dropped from 1,200 people to just 40!

(right) Extra trains were sent to move people out of Gwalia after the mine closed. Townspeople left belongings, such as this automobile, behind.

43

Billabongs

Many parts of the Australian interior have been untouched by human development for millions of years. The rivers that flow here naturally change course over time. When this happens, part of a river that no longer has water flowing through it creates a pond or lake. These ponds or lakes fill up with water during the rainy season, and dry out during the dry season. Australians call them billabongs. Billabongs have traditionally been an important water source for Indigenous Australians, early settlers and travelers, and animals.

(background) Billabongs can be big or small. The word billabong comes from the Indigenous Wiradjuri language and means "dead river." In other parts of the world, billabongs are called oxbow lakes.

FIVE Billabong Animals

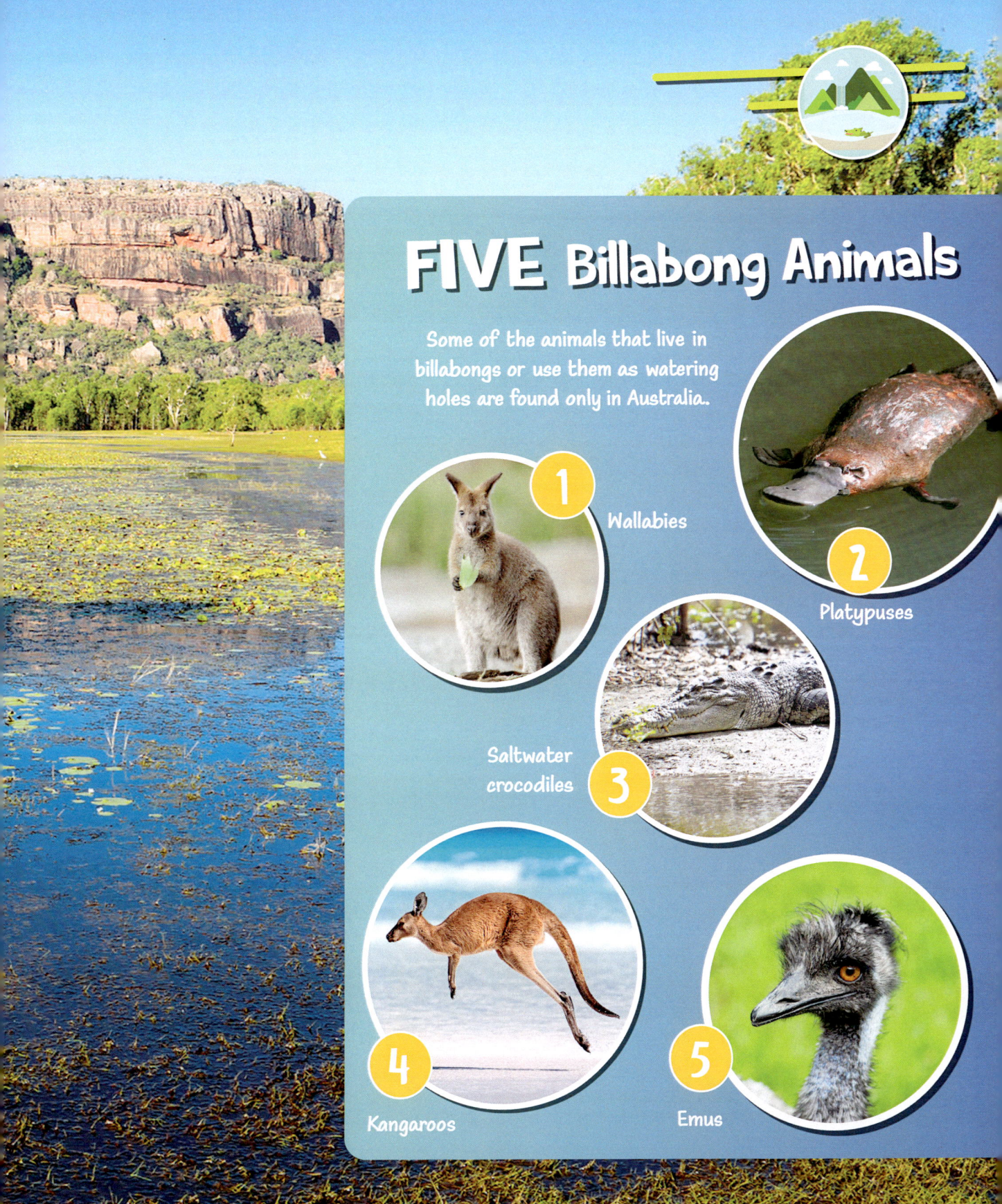

Some of the animals that live in billabongs or use them as watering holes are found only in Australia.

1. Wallabies
2. Platypuses
3. Saltwater crocodiles
4. Kangaroos
5. Emus

Australia at a Glance

Official Name ....Commonwealth of Australia
Population ....26 million
National Animal ....Kangaroo
Currency ....Australian Dollar
Official Language ....English
Size ....2.6 million square miles
.................................(7.6 million square km)

Flag of Australia

Australia is the world's largest island country. It is also a continent. This world map has the other continents labeled and Australia highlighted in red.

Flight time from New York to Australia: Approximately 22 hours.

North America

Europe

Asia

Africa

South America

YOU ARE HERE

AUSTRALIA

Australia has three separate time zones: Australian Eastern Time, Australian Central Time, and Australian Western Time. If you finish school at 3 p.m. on Monday in New York, it is 7 a.m. on Tuesday in Sydney, Australia, and kids there are just getting up for school!

Glossary

Anzac Short for Australian and New Zealand Army Corps, the name of an army unit jointly formed by both countries during WWI (1914-1918).

atmosphere Layers of gases that surround Earth.

British Commonwealth A group of independent countries formerly ruled by Britain that cooperate in trade and support one another in global matters.

colonial government The government of a colony, usually led by a governor appointed by the ruling country.

commemorate To remember and show respect for something.

convict Someone who has been found guilty of a crime and is in prison.

creation stories Traditional stories that cultures have to explain their history, beliefs, and how the world came to be.

engineer A person who designs, builds, or maintains engines, machines, or public works.

erode To wash or wear away, usually by wind or water.

expedition A journey taken by a group of people for exploration or research.

geologist A scientist who studies the surface of Earth and what it is made from.

Indigenous peoples The first peoples of a place.

interior The inside of something.

international exhibition Another word for a world's fair. The period between 1880 and WWI is known as the "golden age" of international exhibitions, which were huge events that promoted inventions, manufacturing, and scientific achievements.

landform A natural feature of Earth's surface, such as mountains, valleys, and plateaus.

mangroves Trees and bushes that grow in clusters along seashores and riverbanks. They have roots that stick up through the mud.

microorganism A tiny living thing that is too small to be seen without a microscope.

minerals Natural, solid substances that make up rocks, sand, and soil.

mythical A word to describe something that is imaginary, or made up.

plantation A very large farm that produces only one type of crop.

plates The surface of Earth is cracked into different pieces called tectonic plates. Plates move and create mountains and earthquakes.

predator An animal that hunts other animals for food.

sacred A word used to describe something that is holy and very respected.

sandstone A type of rock that is formed when grains of sand are compressed together.

seagrass Types of underwater plants that grow like grasses.

sediment Tiny pieces of rocks, minerals, or the remains of dead animals that can be carried by wind or moving water.

Spanish flu A deadly flu pandemic that struck many countries of the world between 1918–19.

species A group of similar living things that are able to reproduce with one another.

stockade A wooden barricade used for defense.

tax Money that people pay to the government, which is then used to run the country.

tramway A trolley or streetcar system within a city or town.

urban A word used to describe areas where many people live and work in close proximity to one another, such as cities and towns.

Learning More

Books

Amazing Landmarks: Discover the hidden stories behind 10 iconic structures! by Rekha S. Rajan. Scholastic Inc., 2022.

Your Passport to Australia (World Passport series) by A.M. Reynolds. Capstone Press, 2022.

Spotlight on Australia by Bobbie Kalman. Crabtree Publishing, 2008.

Websites

Britannica Kids: Visit the Landmarks article to learn about landmarks around the world.
https://kids.britannica.com/kids/article/landmarks-at-a-glance/608620

National Geographic Kids Countries Guides: Find out more about Australia.
www.kids.nationalgeographic.com/geography/countries/article/australia

Globe Trottin' Kids: Country information for kids.
https://www.globetrottinkids.com/countries/australia/

Index

Anzac 40-41

beaches 4, 10, 18-19
Big Things 30-31
boomerangs 12

Canberra 12-13, 40-41
cities 4, 6-7, 12-13, 18-19, 20-21, 26-27, 30, 36-37, 40-41
colony 16, 20, 26
convicts 16-17
coral reefs 10-11

engineering 6-7, 26-27

explorers 24, 28-29

government 12, 15, 20
Great Britain 16, 41

Indigenous peoples 4, 8, 12, 13, 15, 23, 32-33, 44

land animals 4, 9, 13, 30-31, 32, 41, 44-45

Melbourne 12, 20-21, 28, 36-37
mining 20-21, 42-43

mountains 4, 15

Outback 4, 8-9, 22-23, 28-29, 32-33, 38-39, 42-43, 44-45

penal colony 16-17

rivers 44-45
rocks 8-9, 13, 14-15, 22-23, 24, 25, 32, 34-35, 38-39

sea life 7, 10-11, 18, 24-25, 30

sharks 11, 18, 24, 25
sheep 30, 31
statues 4, 30-31
surfing 18, 19
Sydney 6-7, 18-19, 26-27, 46

tourism 10
towers 4, 17, 20-21